60 HABITS FOR HAPPINESS

How to trigger positive emotions

ROXANNE MARTIN

Table of Contents

INTRODUCTION

This book is not an instructional guide; rather it's a self-help book that focuses on how to be happy by cultivating the right habits. You will also learn about the body hormones and neurotransmitters that bring about the feeling of happiness as well as the habits you should have to trigger them.

Happiness is not something you postpone for the future; it is something you design for the present - Jim Rohn

Happiness is more than just a feeling. It defines your life. It is not an involuntary reaction; rather it is a conscious decision. Happiness is the key to a successful career and life. If you are happy with what you are doing, success will come with consistency and self-belief. Intriguingly, this has a direct relationship with our health and it is because when we are happy, our body releases certain anti-stress hormones and other chemicals that trigger antibodies to fight diseases and improve your overall well-being.

True happiness, is an inner quality. It is a state of mind. If your mind is at peace, you are happy. If your mind is at peace, but you have nothing else, you can be happy - Dada Vaswani

Aside from the beneficial chemicals your body, there are hormones in the body that have a direct or indirect influence on our happiness feeling. Once these hormones are triggered, we can experience a mood lift.

We would be discussing how the secretion of these hormones can be increased in the body, as well as how we can develop the right habit to produce and and how to keep this feeling for the rest of our lives. I will also be sharing with you some personal and shared stories on how I have been able to break free from the shackles of self-pity and despondency to embrace the freedom that comes from self-motivation through the change in habits.

CHAPTER ONE

Little Habits that Steal Your Happiness

I had once toiled this road before, I had allowed little habits to steal my happiness. Like the saying goes, "little foxes destroy the vineyard." In this chapter, I will be sharing with you some mistakes and lessons I have learned in life as regards to my habits.

Avid or voracious readers would have read that whatever you do consistently for 21 days becomes part of you. Your habits either help you or ruin you.

Whatever is not making you fulfilled is merely fooling you.

My Story

I grew up with this belief that I was not loved by my parents for trying to force me to choose a career path I never intended to follow. I felt they were too strict and did not allow me the freedom to explore and express myself. Due to my stubborn nature, they took me to a boarding school where they believed

I will learn morals and be well disciplined. They didn't just enroll me in boarding school, they took me to a school controlled by a tough management. Though I mingled with friends of questionable character who were into alcohol and other substances, my stubborn nature had its 100% positive side of not giving into things like that. It is one of the reasons I am grateful for my parents because they tutored me well on the adverse effects of these vices.

I must say that the management of my school really drilled me and my parents were happy that I had been well disciplined. Although, they failed to recognize the seed of bitterness being sown in me. I graduated from high school feeling no one ever loved me. I hoped that the status quo would change and it did.

I had a very wrong mentality, which I felt was right until I started having issues with low self-esteem, depression, anxiety and other emotional issues. Then I met a friend who sneaked into my life unnoticed. He was able to have a positive influence on my life, unlike other friends I have made before that time. He made me understand that I can live happily, stay happy with the right mindset, and do the right things.

First, I had to forgive my parents and let go of the hurt, which I eventually did. This opened up space in my heart for a positive change. Then I began to read and attend seminars on how to live happy to achieve your life's goal. This made me realize some of my mistakes, which I will share with you and how I was able to correct them. Then I also learned about some hormones in our body, which are called happy hormones that help to liven up our moods and make us happy and healthy.

Here, I have highlighted few of the little habits that can steal your happiness, ultimately erode you of your sound health, and debar you from experiencing success.

Focusing on other people's story while neglecting your own

Are you contented with listening to the success stories of others? Do you care so much about how they have made it at the expense of not writing your own?

Let people know about your story too. You possess all the prerequisites to become what you are capable of becoming. Change only occurs when the pain of leaving where you are is more than the pain it will cost you to move on, it starts with your decision to take control.

In the world, it means creating more and consuming less, refusing to allow others decide for you. It also has to do with learning to respect and write your story based on your ideas.

To write a soul-lifting life story, you need to chart a new

course, reduce time wastages and burdens that weigh you down, and pick up the things that motivate you. Keep your greatest goals and wishes close to your heart and allocate time to them daily. A consistent and modicum diligence and focus will cause you to accomplish anything.

Waiting for the perfect moment

Don't allow yourself to be deceived by the term perfect moment. There aren't perfect moments anywhere, moments are what you make of them. So many people believe the stars will one day align, thereby allowing them to do that special thing. People often believe in the myth perfect moment, opportunity, etc. Wake up from your slumber! These states of perfection are mere fables. They do not exist.

Your ability to grow to attain the utmost potential has a direct relationship to your willingness to act in the face of imperfection. Success doesn't come by finding a perfect moment, but by perfectly learning to make use of life's imperfections perfectly.

Working for nothing more than a paycheck

"Work without interest is imprisonment." While your passion

for your work might not be superlative, you still need to be interested in it at least.

When your life is founded on the lifestyle of working to pay up your bills, you will eventually end up being frustrated while you try your best to be like someone else. Your work will definitely eat up a large chunk of your time and life. Money is not the only important thing, your life is more important.

Ignore the false statements, such as "Never let your work define you." Rephrase and meditate on this statement: "I will do the work that defines me." Fulfillment is being achieved when you naturally self-define at least some part of the work you do for a living.

Conclusively, having good interest in your work guarantees you a quality output and happiness of mind. Don't just work to get a paycheck that barely sustains you, rather search around until you get a work that interests you.

Harboring feelings of hate

"Darkness cannot drive out darkness; only light can do that. Hate cannot drive out hate; only love can do that." - Martin Luther King Jr

Harbored feelings of hate will eventually get the best of us and control us. We reach a point where we tend to forget why, what, and whom we hate – we simply hate for hating sake. In addition, we naturally start to hate ourselves.

If you want to live a happy life, do not hate, as it does you no good. It only robs you of tomorrow's strength.

Holding tight to worries and fears

Someday when you take a retrospective look at your life, you'll realize that nearly all your fears, worries, and anxiety never came to a realization – they were completely unfounded. Therefore, why not start understanding this fact right now that worries don't improve you but only leads to sadness and not happiness. Looking back over the past few years, how many joyful opportunities did you destroy with your worries and negativity, which are needless and baseless?

Although you can't do anything about these lost joys, you can still do a lot of other ones that will soon come your way. You will come to the realization that it's better to let go of some things simply because they're heavy on your heart. Let go of them. Take the shackles off your feet. It's much easier to enjoy your life right now, no matter the situation attached to it. It's just a matter of the things weighing you down.

Let go of all your worries, fears, rage, jealousy and the domineering attitude of yours. Understand that things can't always go your way, you need to accept in silence the minor aggravations.

You find happiness and fulfillment underneath all these layers of nonsensical attitude. When you eliminate them from your life and start appreciating everything for what it is, life can be happy and fulfilling.

Dwelling on difficulties

We all have bad days, but learn to recognize a bad day as simply a bad day. Don't make it anything more! Life is full of vicissitudes and we will all have these moments. Though adverse times will definitely affect your living conditions including your work, yet you shouldn't let it affect who you are and your destination.

Adjust to the setbacks that you experience in life, but don't aggravate them by making them a key part of your life. New lessons and possibilities come each day.

Despite all odds, there will always be a way forward on your chosen path. At times, events may be terrible, but there is always a choice.

Constantly seeking fleeting contentment

Contentment in life comes in two types "fleeting and enduring." The fleeting type comes from the experience of material comfort, while the enduring type is experienced through the continuous mind growth. It might seem difficult to distinguish one from the other, but the difference starts getting obvious over time as the enduring contentment is greater than the fleeting one.

Enduring contentment is sustained through life's challenges because your mind remains at peace and confident through this challenges.

Conversely, the fleeting changes of life have the ability to disturb your mind to the extent that even the most sophisticated physical comforts won't do much to increase your happiness for long periods of time.

Trying to make a big difference all at once

You need to be different to make a difference in the world. You also need to start with the world around you. Nevertheless, it's almost impossible to make a big difference all at once as it's an extremely stressful process.

However, it's quite possible and easy to make an instant difference in a few lives. All you need is to focus on one person at a time starting with the closest people to you.

Work to make some money and try spreading it around a bit. Sometimes, for you to change a person's mind, you will need to first change the minds of the people around them. For example, a smile is contagious. Therefore, if you make a person to smile, their smile might also affect others and make them smile too.

Holding on to someone who is toxic

Sometimes the best way to be happy is to walk away from toxic people because they don't care and not because you don't care. When someone is hurting you repeatedly, admit the fact that he or her does not care about you and do not expect them to change. Life is short and people rarely change at their core.

Toxic people are those who have sudden mood changes, they are happy one moment and a few seconds later they are angry or miserable about some insignificant incident. They make you feel good for a short while but most of the time when you have them around you are sad and miserable, because they don't appreciate you.

Do not bother trying to impress or further prove something to them. Live as if they do not exist.

CHAPTER TWO

Simple Things You Can Do Every Day to Be Consistently Happy

After reading about the little habits that can limit your happiness in the previous chapter, we need to now learn about the simple things you can do every day to be consistently happy. As we have discussed, it takes a conscious effort to be happy and it doesn't take many complex things to be happy. It starts with little steps.

Self-discovery is one of the important steps to a happy life. For instance, one important thing I've learned is that I am at my best performance when I'm happy. I find it easier to stay focused when I am happy.

I've found few key habits which act as great ritual that enables me to be consistently happy. They also serve to support all other activities to quickly raise my level of happiness whenever I don't feel 100%.

So here are some of the things I do:

1. **Wake up early**

Whether you work for someone or you have your personal business, learn to wake early. From the little experiment I have done on my daily routine, I realized that when you wake up early, you feel more energized, invigorated and happy which helps to set a good pace for the day's activities.

I have found over time that I accomplish my daily task at a higher pace in the morning than any other time of the day. So, most of the time, I crave for that "early morning" feeling whereby I can be focused enough to do some great work.

I love to wake up as early as 6:00 a.m. every day of the week even on vacation because I love it. When you do what you love, the result can only be success and happiness.

It takes discipline to wake up early every day. In addition, do not forget that waking up early is a function of the time you wind up for the day. Therefore, I have a daily routine of disengaging from daily activities at about 9:30 pm while I sleep at 10 pm. I enjoy every aspect of this new habit and I wake up at 6 am feeling fresh and ready to achieve my daily goals.

On the average, you will have about 25,000 mornings in your

lifetime, so there is room for a lot of experiment.

2. Daily exercise

"Physically active people have more pleasant-activated feelings than less active people"

Recently, I've done some intermittent and erratic exercise schedule to make it part of my daily routine. At the beginning, I had little idea of how a gym operated, so I asked a friend, who's a personal trainer. I then visited the gym a couple of times with him and soon I was hooked.

Over time, this was developed into a habit so strong that I just can't do without it, and through consistency, I feel happy and can easily take on more challenges.

I recently discovered that exercise is a key precursor to most happiness hormones in the body. When you exercise, you will feel happy because certain "happy hormones" are being released. I've also discovered that exercise helps me sleep well each night.

3. Have a habit of disengagement

As earlier mentioned, one of the major reason why I can easily wake at 6 am is the habit of disengaging from daily activities in the evening. At 9:30 pm, I set out for a walk along familiar routes that I've walked several times. Since it's a defined route, all I do is simply walking and nothing else. This prompts relaxation and reflection.

Various thoughts come to mind while others leave my mind during the walk, and I have discovered that it has improved me health-wise.

My thoughts run to the unfortunate incident of the day if there is any and how I can handle it better some other time to be happier. Other times I think about the great things that happened that day which I enjoy.

When I get back home from my walk, I feel more calm and relaxed and I can, therefore, retire to bed and fall asleep.

4. **Help others regularly**

I personally discovered that I experience more happiness when I help others to be happy. Helping others also triggers certain happy hormones, which will be discussed in subsequent chapters. Happiness is what you give and it keeps coming back to you. Choose today to make someone happy.

5. Learn new skills

Learning new skills and undertaking new challenges makes you to be happy. For each accomplished goal of learning new skills comes a burst of happiness.

It may seem odd that new challenges can amount to happiness, but it is the fact. You don't feel happy doing what doesn't challenge you, rather you feel happy accomplished challenging tasks.

One key reason why the acquisition of new skills can bring happiness is that, to make significant progress, you will engage your brain to focus. This triggers the release of some happy hormones in your body.

CHAPTER THREE

5 Ways to Boost Happy Hormones

One major consequence of living in a computer age is that you get more detached from having physical activities due to spending more time on social media and your body is almost short-circuiting. Balancing of neurochemicals and hormones, which was developed several years ago, has been altered by the modern lifestyle. This makes you more prone to depression and anxiety.

The Pharmaceutical companies aim to readjust this trend with pills. However, I won't be prescribing a drug for boosting your happy hormones, rather I will prescribe simple lifestyle choices that'll help to improve your brain chemistry and cause changes in your behavior and happiness level.

With these tips, you will be better motivated to maximize your human potential.

6. Spend time with friends

Your oxytocin (love hormone) level is triggered by the trust.

Spending quality time with positive minded people will raise your happiness level. Being grateful and talking about the good things in life also increases your happiness. Using good moments with friends and laughing boosts your happy hormones.

Those people that remain in a happy mood usually have strong relationship ties and they are more social. When you are happy, your friend becomes happy as a good friend, because happiness is contagious. One study says in 2011, that spending time with your friends reduces your level of stress.

At times, your friend may turn out to be your best exercise buddy too. When you make a decision to achieve your aim and later achieve them, you can increase your levels of dopamine hormone.

Relating to others will make you to be more compassionate. Scientists opine that your spirit can be lifted through the release of oxytocin in your body by making new friends. Your friend doesn't just increase your happy hormones, but a plus is that scientifically it assist you to live longer.

7. **Exercise**

Improving self-esteem is also the key psychological benefit of regular physical activity. Doing exercise boosts most of the happy hormones. Doing any form of exercise will increase your happy hormones. It can be by:

- Dancing
- Jogging
- Gardening
- Walking
- Playing tennis
- Yoga
- Housework especially vacuuming, mopping or sweeping
- Yard work especially raking or moving
- Low impact aerobics
- Biking

You can benefit from joining a group exercise class. You will enter into a state of heightened focus, which releases the bliss molecule anandamide when you do exercise. When you start to exercise, dopamine, endorphins, serotonin, norepinephrine, and progesterone are all triggered. Doing some training also provides you with these added benefits:

- Strengthens your heart
- Lowers blood pressure

- Improves muscle strength and tone
- Build and strengthens bones
- Make you healthy and fit
- Help reduce body fat
- It increases your energy level.

8. **Meditate**

The most invaluable gift that you can give to yourself is meditation. The daily demands and hustle of life can eventually have a toll on your life. When meditating, you can obtain happiness, peace of mind and joy, self-friendship, clarity, and insight.

Meditation can trigger the release of GABA, estrogen, serotonin, and anandamide.

9. **Diet**

Your brain needs nutrients that like folate, iron and vitamin B12 to make the neurotransmitters like dopamine, norepinephrine, and serotonin to function optimally. Eating something poor increases the risk of brain disorders like depression and dementia and shrinks your brain.

Rules of Happy Diet

You should lower the amount of processed food you eat. You should eat more fruits, veggies, and whole grains. Opt for grass-fed meat because this is very rich in omega three fatty acids. Strive for variety, the more the whole foods that you consume, the happier and energized your mind will be. Likewise, the more brain-boosting nutrients you have in your diet, the sharper your brain becomes.

Foods that Increase Your Happiness

Foods for energy: Coffee, blue or red-skinned potatoes, Arugula, and walnuts.

Foods for good mood: Tomatoes, garlic, wild salmon and beets Chile peppers.

Foods for thought: Grass-fed butter, anchovies, grass-fed beef, and eggs.

10. **Aromatherapy**

The smell doesn't have a strong impact on any of your other senses except your brain. Most time when you take the sniff of the right aroma, you can change the form of your mood. When you feel depressed and uninterested, you should apply aromatherapy to help kick-start happy hormones production.

Scents that boost happy hormones

There are certain scents known to help boost the secretion of happy hormones in the body in order to help boost your happiness level.

Among such is the citrus scents that give your brain new energy. It also helps to lighten up one's mood. The effects of lime, oranges, grapefruit or lemon are similar. Geranium scent reduces your stress and anxiety. During the day, when things are becoming stressful, and you still have a lot to do, geranium can put you in a better frame of mind. Basil and rosemary help to increase your focus level.

These are the best choices when you're studying, thinking, or working. Allspice cloves and cinnamon both have a spicy scent that is eye-opening and vitalizing. When you use these scents early in the morning, they are the best to improve your energy.

Research also shows that people who had aromatherapy massages alongside listening to music had their anxiety level significantly reduced.

Happiness is the most important element in your overall

health. Aside from the five ways to boost your happy hormones, these are some of the science-backed ways to increase your happiness.

11. Quit Facebook for a month. People that left Facebook for a week reportedly experienced an increase in their average happiness rating.

Looking at the cute animals on your way to work, planning a vacation to distant places, doing charitable deeds, spending quality time with positive and happy people, getting a good night sleep, and listening to great music improves your feeling of happiness.

You may think that happiness is somehow hard to achieve if you know the steps to take. These are all simple to achieve. Try out these tips and see for yourself.

CHAPTER FOUR

Happy Hormones

Happiness comes because of our emotions that vary from the feeling of contentment to intense joy. The joyful feeling is being experienced when certain chemicals are being released by your brain. These chemicals are called neurotransmitters.

Happiness Hormones

Our body system is designed in such a way that it does all the necessary things for your survival and tries to make you feel good. Your brain has an abundance of self-produced neurochemicals that turns life struggles into pleasure and increases your happiness when you achieve them.

Aside from the happy hormones in our body, we also have certain chemicals in the brain called neurotransmitters, which is also responsible for the happy feeling. When these neurotransmitters are released, they help to transmit messages from one neuron to another nerve.

In this book, we will discuss extensively on nine brain molecules that influence happiness and how they can be released. You will learn about hormones and neurotransmitters that will make you happy.

The main difference between hormones and neurotransmitters is that hormones are associated with your endocrine system while neurotransmitters are associated with your nervous system.

Here is the list of happiness hormones available in our bodies along with brief details of their functions.

- Dopamine

This is also known as the reward hormone, as it provides the motivation and impetus needed to take action towards achieving your goals. It then gives you a surge of pleasure when you achieve the set goals. If your dopamine level is low, you may begin to experience lack of enthusiasm, self-doubt, and procrastination.

Research shows that if dopamine is too much or too little, it could pose serious health. For instance, producing too little dopamine molecules can lead to Parkinson's disease while excess production can lead to hallucinations and schizophrenia. Therefore, it needs to be at moderate levels in the body.

Let there be a consistent release of dopamine by breaking down big goals into small attainable ones. Instead of celebrating when you complete a task, create a series of a little endpoint.

Don't be left with dopamine after-effect. Try setting new goals once you near completion of the current one. With that, a constant stream of dopamine will be ensured.

- Oxytocin

This is known as a bonding hormone as it links directly with bonding in humans. The presence of this hormone increases trust while reducing anxiety and stress. Oxytocin also helps people with autism to improve their social functioning.

One of the most effective ways to trigger oxytocin is through physical intimacy such as a hug. That is why it is called the cuddle hormone. Oxytocin level is directly related to your happiness level as the higher it is, the higher your happiness and well-being especially for women.

- Endorphin

Endorphins translate into a self-produced painkiller. Endorphin is being released in response to pain and stress. The presence of endorphin also helps to reduce anxiety and depression. Endorphin is responsible for the rushing "second wind" and ecstatic "runners high" being experienced from an energetic run.

- Anandamide

This is an endocannabinoid otherwise referred to as bliss molecule and it is part of the body's neurotransmitter that is produced in your brain. The name "bliss molecule" is synonymous with bliss, joy or happiness, as it is known to bring such.

Anandamide's role goes beyond the provision of heightened happiness as it also plays a major role in pain reduction, appetite, and fertility. Anandamide comprises of anti-anxiety and anti-depressant properties, which helps to increase new cell formation.

Including more of chocolate especially dark chocolate in your diet will further boost anandamide level thereby leading to super concentration and top performance.

- GABA

GABA is an anti-anxiety molecule, which is an important neurotransmitter in your brain. It decreases nerve transmission by giving your neurons more time to recover. GABA neurotransmitter reduces anxiety and thereby creates a sense of calmness. It also enhances your focus and helps you maintain control. Practicing yoga and meditation helps to increase naturally the GABA molecule.

- Serotonin

Serotonin secretion stems from the feeling of importance and significance. When you lack serotonin, you often suffer from loneliness and depression. You can overcome depression by trying to reflect on your achievements. Your brain may not be able to differentiate effectively the difference between real and imagined experience so, it starts producing serotonin. Serotonin boosts your self-esteem, fights depression and improves sleep.

- Norepinephrine

The rush of adrenaline is attributed to norepinephrine molecule. That's why it's called the energy molecule. Norepinephrine is a stress hormone involved in the fight or flight response. Its presence set the tone for many of the physical components of emotion such as cognition, decision-making, increased heart rate, and alertness.

Rigorous exercise helps to improve your level of norepinephrine. Also, ensure you eat balanced meals containing whole grains, lean protein, and vegetables.

CHAPTER FIVE

How To Release Happy Hormones

As we have discussed in the previous chapter, we have several hormones and neurotransmitters that are actively involved in our general wellbeing, as well as raising our happiness level. Here is an in-depth information on the hormones and neurotransmitters responsible for our happy feeling.

1. ENDORPHINS

Endorphin is one of the most important happiness hormones in our body. It's been produced in our body's pituitary gland. Its major function is to cause a lasting satisfaction, happiness and alleviate pain sensation. Endorphins function as a natural painkiller or pain mask.

Endorphins help to elevate and enhance your mood by creating a feeling of euphoria. The more endorphins your body is able to produce, the happier you will be. Endorphin is a chemical substance released in the instance of pain or stress. Its secretion helps to alleviate depression and anxiety. It is common knowledge that exercise helps to release endorphins. However, not all realize why it is so.

History has it that endorphins use became prominent during the Stone Age while our ancestors needed to escape from predators. It helps them to keep running through the pain during a hot chase from predators.

Nowadays, we do not have any predators to escape from neither do we need to chase after a predator. Therefore, endorphins are only produced when anaerobic exercises are performed, as it helps us to keep running even when our oxygen stores are depleted.

Aside from just the natural instinct of producing endorphins through aerobics, it is imperative that you know the other ways at which endorphins are released from the body. This will help you to trigger and access its numerous advantages when needed for happiness and ameliorating pain.

How to Release the Happy Hormone "Endorphin"

12. Physical activities

As earlier discussed, physical exercise is the basic precursor of endorphin. Findings reveal that those who engage in regular exercise experience increase in endorphin release than those who do not.

Endorphin released during physical activities such as running is responsible for a sensation known as "runner's high," whereby an individual engaging in physical activity experiences happiness right in the middle of a strenuous exercise. Choose a dynamic sport that you enjoy very much, like Zumba or Aerobics and your endorphin level will surely be increased.

We all move our body daily, but we do not all release endorphin as much as is required to have this happy feeling. This is because the body is designed such that just ordinary body movement will not release endorphin except you engage in either extensive muscle training or cardiovascular exercises. This is when the pituitary gland can be more stimulated to release the endorphin substance in good quantity for maximum benefit.

Rigorous exercise releases endorphin, which activates our body's natural painkillers and enables us to cope with chronic pains. Another advantage of physical exercise is that it helps your organ system function properly as it makes you feel healthier.

When endorphins secretion is increased, it will lead to a feeling of happiness and self-contentment. When our muscles are depleted of glycogen through rigorous exercise, endorphins helps us to push on. This is why we only feel pain or blisters after the exercise not during the exercise.

A study revealed that group exercise is a more effective way to increase endorphin level. Aside from the fact that it provides one with a support system during your workout, it also boosts the release of endorphin.

13. Chocolate

Taking chocolate is another method of triggering the release of endorphin. Have you ever wondered why our parents do give kids chocolate whenever the child feels emotional or distressed? Perhaps, they may see it as a normal thing to do and they might not place any significance on it. However, there are several benefits of doing that. One may think it makes the child feel happy after enjoying the taste of the chocolate. This reason is not totally out of place as the calming effect after eating chocolate has a scientific backing.

Endorphins release are being triggered by eating chocolates which will, in turn, trigger the emotions of joy and pleasure to be generated from the brain. Sweet chocolates also contain phenylethylamine (PEA) which is a feel-good effect chemical substance.

14. Spicy dishes

Aside from taking chocolate, consumption of spicy foods also plays a vital role in the release of endorphin.

Once your tongue receptors feel the spiciness of the food, it automatically sends a signal to the brain similar to pain signal thereby triggering the release of happy hormones endorphin. The spicier your food is, the more stimulated your nerve cells are to release endorphins.

15. Alcohol

The intake of alcohol also stimulates endorphin release. This is why some people indulge in the drinking of alcohol, as they believe it will help them escape their problems.

Whenever someone faces a debilitating situation or becomes too stressed, taking alcohol will help the person relax while taking his or her mind off reality. In fact, endorphin is released in response to alcohol consumption.

However, note that too much alcohol could affect the brain structure of heavy drinkers, thereby making alcohol more pleasurable and addictive to them. During alcohol-induced endorphin release, someone is likely to develop an addiction to alcohol due to excessive release of endorphins.

16. Smiling

This is quite funny but it's a fact that smiling could actually help release the happy hormone endorphin. When one smiles, the facial muscles will be stretched automatically thereby causing the muscle movements to trigger the brain into producing endorphins.

Smiling doesn't only lighten up your mood, it also helps to free your inner stress. Therefore, when you a bit low, one easy way to lighten up the mood is by smiling. Even when you do not feel like smiling, you could give a fake smile just to keep smiling. You will definitely have yourself to thank after smiling because you will definitely feel better once endorphin is released.

17. Meditation

Happy hormones can also be released via meditation. One of the common meditation exercises is practicing yoga. One of the advantages of yoga is its role in the reduction of stress because of endorphin release. Another reason why yoga is good for endorphin release to the body is its controlled breathing exercise. The endorphin takes the role of a natural analgesic and kills the pain.

18. Vanilla Scent

Research has it that vanilla scent also contributes to the release of endorphin. It was noted that vanilla scent could actually reduce the rate of anxiety in people as endorphin level is increased after a few drops of vanilla extract.

19. Lavender

Most of the times when I feel depressed or uncomfortable with myself I spray my room with a lavender fragrance and the calming effect it gives to me is so refreshing. Its lovely scent stimulates endorphin production; it helps to decrease depression and insomnia. A lavender extract can also be applied to the wrist, neck, or temples such that the scent can easily diffuse through the nasal opening and cause an inspiration of some sort.

20. Ginseng

Ginseng is well-known for its role in controlling blood sugar and weight reduction. However, those feeling sluggish or inactive can use ginseng as it enhances endorphin production. Ginseng works by enhancing the production of "feel-good" hormone while blocking the release of stress hormones.

Since it helps to maintain the normal functioning of the cardiovascular, nervous and respiratory system, an individual feels ecstatic thereby leading to a positive feedback and the release of endorphins.

21. Laughter

The happy hormone endorphin can be released through laughter. In fact, it's one of the easiest ways to increase endorphin level after regular exercise. This is more natural than using herbs like ginseng.

According to researchers, people who are accustomed to laughter do release more endorphin daily than those who do not.

Other statistics have it that children who laugh approximately 300 times per day release more endorphins when compared with adults who only laugh about 5 times daily. Therefore, you are urged to inculcate laughing with friends as part of your daily routine. Aside from helping you to release stress, it will also help increase endorphins level in your system.

Have you ever wondered how you feel when you attend a comedy show or you are around a friend who likes to crack your ribs with laughter? You feel so happy, elated, excited, and euphoria. This is because your endorphin has been stimulated so you feel so good about yourself. Needless to mention the several health benefits you will enjoy from having a good sense of humor.

Since we now know that laughing contributes to the increase of endorphin levels, we might also be tempted to think that crying has the opposite effect. However, this is not so as crying also promotes the release of endorphin because an immediate relief and calmness are experienced after an emotional break down of tears. This increases the level of endorphin in the body.

22. Sex

We feel a high rate of excitement and ecstasy during a sex romp. This is attributed to the increase in endorphin release. Sex helps to balance your feel-good hormone level and increases joy and satisfaction.

A moment of sex and intimacy with your partner reduces tension and enhances your mood greatly.

23. Natural happiness

Finally, finding happiness naturally by staying optimistic and being positive is one of the most effective ways to release endorphin. When you stay positive and optimistic, you will become happier and more relaxed with your life. For a simple and faster way of endorphin release, ensure you maintain a positive outlook on life.

Final note

Endorphin is a natural way of releasing pain, making us feel happy, and helping us rise from depression.

We should take note of these precursors of endorphin and not make ourselves addicted to it in a bid to trigger its release, as too much of it can affect us.

For example, if we try to mask our pain with endorphin release all the time, we would end up with a serious injury because we have pushed our bodies too hard. Therefore, moderation is key in all you do in order to stay happy and healthy.

2. **OXYTOCIN**

Oxytocin is an important hormone in the body that is released by the pituitary gland in the brain. When released, it produces satisfaction, happiness and a feeling of love. The secretion of this love hormone makes new mothers to form a loving bond with their newborn babies.

The presence of oxytocin can be felt in certain body organs, which includes the breasts, uterus and the reproductive system.

Oxytocin release has been attributed to behaviors such as love, trust, and sexual arousal. It is released when there is a physical contact with the ones you love. Oxytocin helps to build also immunity as well as building trust in relationships.

When one is happy, oxytocin is then released into the bloodstream due to electrical activity of nerve cells.

This hormone always works by a positive feedback system. At anywhere the oxytocin is released more will be produced. This also explains how the more a baby breastfeeds, the more breast milk the mother produces. Oxytocin level can also be increased when one receives a gift from friends and loved ones.

Habits for releasing the Happy Hormone "Oxytocin"

24. Physical Contact

Kisses, cuddling, and hugs, increase oxytocin levels quickly. Men's reaction to sex shows that they are under the control of oxytocin. Oxytocin is released when you have an orgasm and for men, it is only released when they are with someone they love.

25. Words of Encouragement

Anytime we hear a word of encouragement, we always feel good about ourselves. We have the belief that we are being loved and held in high regard, so it leads to happiness.

The best way to cheer yourself is to try to cheer someone else up - Mark Twain

Oxytocin increases when caring for others or when we are being cared for. Spoken words do have a soothing effect and when we feel loved and we react to it, oxytocin level is increased.

26. Listen

Everybody wants to feel accepted and heard. Listening is a unique way to increase oxytocin. Listen carefully. Close the computer. Drop the phone. Create time to be more intimate with another. You will find a sense of belonging that is precious.

27. Laugh and Smile

Have you ever noticed how children play? They smile and laugh a lot thereby releasing loads of oxytocin. It's quite easy to transmit laughter and once it's triggered, it will surely spread like wildfire. Research has it that health is improved through smiling and laughing. It occurs subconsciously at most times. People who are always excited have their oxytocin released all the time. Laughter makes a sense of joy that is the biggest trade-off in life.

28. Meditation

Anytime when you pray and relax, your hormones are balanced. Oxytocin also increases when you are not in the flight mode or fight. Meditation and prayer help your mind to overcome stress. It lowers blood pressure and helps the body to feel more balanced. Body, spirit, and mind find a way to relate. Make sure you create time for it at some point in the day. You can meditate for five minutes or more anywhere to release this hormone.

29. Exercise

Oxytocin increase when we do more exercise. The oxygen moves to the brain and to the other parts of our bodies. Exercise is not just for keeping your body fit and functioning properly. The aggregate of hormones released to the brain is also helpful. You may not go to a gym center but jogging, walking around the block or doing soft yoga can bring on these advantages as well.

Aside from relaxing your muscles, having a body massage will increase your emotional wellbeing because a physical contact for a prolonged period will facilitate the release of oxytocin in your system.

30. Crying

Studies have shown that withholding your cry lowers oxytocin levels. Withholding your emotions and not dealing with them effects stress and other physical issues in the body. Your emotional state ought to be balanced with your physical and spiritual bodies. The release of tears helps the body to return to a state of silence as it prevents it from leading to anger or annoyance.

31. Giving

We always feel good whenever we give, volunteer and do for others. Give to charity, give gifts, give your time and give thanks.

If you want others to be happy, practice compassion. If you want to be happy, practice compassion - Dalai Lama

Appreciation and compassion is a huge factor in how we feel. Learn to give and watch how amazing you will feel. Oxytocin produces the happy emotions with others. Giving brings a sense of fulfillment and happiness that triggers oxytocin.

32. Get Creative

Creativity helps to reduce the stress on the mental mind. While you are being creative, you aren't fearing or worrying about anything. As you try to act your hobby such as drawing, writing, or playing an instrument, you are helping the feel-good hormone to take control of the brain. Making out time to indulge in your talents is a great way to be happy.

33. Get a Pet

Animals also have a way of making us feel happy. For instance, when you enter the house, your dog and cat are restless waiting for you to give them love. The same feeling of oxytocin release you get when you touch another person is also applicable when you play with your pets. Research tells us that just touching your pets help in lowering your blood pressure and helps to increase your oxytocin levels.

Final note

Oxytocin is a perfect way to build a great relationship, but you need to be careful of who you fall in love with, as you will be heartbroken if you decide to love and trust everyone you meet.

Have you ever imagined how you feel when you hug your loved ones, you feel happy right? That is the work of oxytocin hormone. Once it is released, your cardiovascular stress will be reduced. From now on, instead of you going for a mere handshake, consider a hug.

3. ACETYLCHOLINE

Another great happiness hormone is the acetylcholine that helps in mental and memory alertness, appetite control, and sexual performance. Acetylcholine is a chemical situated around the nerve cells. When triggered, it leads to the skeletal muscles contraction.

Acetylcholine is a neurotransmitter and the role of acetylcholine can be compared to that of a mailperson who goes to deliver mails to each resident's mailbox. Without him, they cannot receive any mail. Just like a mailperson who has many people to deliver mail to and so doesn't waste much time with a particular person, so also is acetylcholine as it acts quickly and does not hang around.

Acetylcholine plays a vital role in reducing the sensation of pain and regulating the endocrine system. When our bodies produce too little acetylcholine, it often degenerates into serious medical complications and we feel weak.

How to Release the Happy Hormone "Acetylcholine"

34. Eat choline-rich food

Acetylcholine is produced from choline, which is an essential nutrient, and the only way to obtain this nutrient is through your diet. It is an essential nutrient needed by your body. Food rich in choline will help maintain the right balance of acetylcholine in your body. When choline is ingested into the body, a certain enzyme helps you transform it into acetylcholine.

The recommended daily intake of choline is 550 mg for male adults and 425 mg for female adults. Choline deficiency may also lead to decrease in the acetylcholine levels thereby affecting the liver, heart and nerve health.

35. Choline-Rich Foods

Most major protein food sources contain a high level of choline. Among them includes dairy, poultry, meats, and fish. The liver contains the highest choline level. Other sources include chocolate, peanut butter, wheat, broccoli and Brussels sprouts.

36. Training exercise

Eating more choline-rich food is not sufficient to increase the level of acetylcholine release in the body. Therefore, you could also include training exercises such as lifting the heavy weight as this increases the number of nerves in the muscle. With the right choline diet and exercise, you can be sure to trigger an increased level of acetylcholine and make you feel happier than you could ever imagine.

Final note

Acetylcholine is great for your mental awareness as it helps to calm your nerves. You need to have adequate knowledge of food substances that could provide it in abundance.

4. DOPAMINE

There are about 86 billion nerve cells in the human brain and they all communicate with themselves via brain chemicals that are called neurotransmitters.

Dopamine is one of the most widely studied neurotransmitters because they are linked to so many ways of human behavior including pleasure seeking, addictions and motivation. It plays useful roles in memory, mood, pleasure, attention, movement, learning, and sleep.

Dopamine that fails to function is the cause of a handful of diseases, with a notable one called Parkinson's disease that is caused by the death of dopamine-producing cells. Relatively few nerve cells make and create dopamine and those that do are present in a few areas of the brain.

Dopamine is also used outside the central nervous system such as the pancreas, immune cells, and kidneys.

This dopamine is made and created locally since it doesn't move freely across the brain's protective blood-brain barrier.

Dopamine Deficiency Symptoms

When you are low on dopamine, you'll have small and little joy for life. Your motivation and energy level will be low while you will frequently rely on sugar, caffeine, or other stimulants to get energy for the day.

Here is a list of common deficiency symptoms of dopamine:

Fatigue

Apathy

Low libido

Sleep problem

Hopelessness

Lack of motivation

Procrastination

Inability to connect with others

Inability to feel pleasure

Mood swings

Memory loss

Inability to concentrate

Dopamine deficiency may also manifest as sure and certain psychiatric disorders including attention deficit disorder (ADD), bipolar disorder, depression, and addictions of all kinds.

How to Release the Happy Hormone "Dopamine"

37. Discover New Things

Dopamine production is triggered when we see something exciting and new in front of us. Our ancestor would experience it when discovering new plants to harvest or new herds to hunt. Unless you're a naturalist, it's likely going to be difficult and hard to do those things. However, we do have the internet.

The internet is a treasure trove for discovering and making research of new videos to new music. Simply browsing Pinterest or even Amazon for new items and products can boost dopamine. However, it will also get addictive so you should make sure you limit your time on websites like these.

38. List Down Your Small Tasks

Dopamine is also released when you finish something, whether it's a small task or a big job. Therefore, it follows that when you want and need more dopamine "hits", you should break down your jobs into bits.

39. Listen to Music

Studies have shown that when you listen to music you actually enjoy, the brain releases dopamine as a response. Even the anticipation of listening to music also increases the level of dopamine in the body, which is the reason why almost everyone loves music.

40. Increase Your Tyrosine

The building block of dopamine is tyrosine and having sufficient tyrosine will benefit you immensely. Fortunately, the food sources of tyrosine are abundant in nature.

These are some common foods sources of tyrosine:

Avocados

Beef

Almonds

Bananas

Yogurt

Milk

Watermelon

Chicken

Eggs

Chocolate

Green Tea

Coffee

I'm very sure you have sufficient knowledge and the right quantity of these in your diet and some of these are foods you must enjoy.

41. Reduce Your Lipopolysaccharides and go for probiotic foods.

Liposaccharide is a difficult word to write, spell and pronounce but that is a good thing, as you need to avoid it as much as you can.

They can also be called endotoxins. When you have too much in the body, it will affect your immune system. Notable among its effect is that it restrains the production of dopamine. The best way to fight this is by having more beneficial bacteria in your intestine.

To achieve this, you should take more probiotic foods, mostly fermented foods like yogurt, kimchi, and kefir. You should get enough sleep so your intestine can keep up with you.

Don't overindulge in sugary and fatty foods. The name says that it's built from polysaccharides and lipids, so less of those means fewer toxins in the body.

42. Exercise Frequently

I've already written much about how exercise assists you to reduce stress and make you super-productive. This is because the physical action is something that your body craves. To make it fun for you, your brain truthfully releases fun chemicals like endorphins, serotonin, and dopamine. The great thing is even non-strenuous exercise can assist in increasing dopamine levels.

Final Note

The importance of dopamine as an effective happiness hormone can't be overemphasized as its deficiency in the body has led to various sickness. The good news is that it could be increased in the body via several food sources alongside regular exercise. Avoid fatty foods; rather go for foods rich in tyrosine and you will experience a boost in your dopamine as well as happiness level.

5. ENKEPHALIN

Enkephalin is a natural hormone that helps to alleviate pain. Enkephalin is closely associated with beta-endorphins, which were discovered to contain a powerful sedation property, and performs a narcotic action.

Enkephalins have strong sedative properties and it's quick release during severe psychological injury cause absence of pain in the affected person. Enkephalin is a hormone that makes one to experience euphoria when running a long-distance race.

How to Release the Happy Hormone "Enkephalin"

43. Get some sun

You may be aware of the mechanism by which your body uses the sun's UVB (Ultraviolet Blue) rays in creating Vitamin D. This is useful for bone health as Vitamin D unlocks your body's capacity to assimilate calcium.

The sunlight also increases your skin's capacity to produce endorphins, which fire up your opioid receptors.

About 30 minutes of direct sunlight, obstruction by windows or UVB blocking sunscreen, is sufficient to make the hormones that can reduce your body's pain response. So you should open a window and bask in the sun, make sure you go for a walk, or you should simply sit and read while the sun allows you to feel good in more ways than one.

44. Take a Cold Shower

Cold-water bath is believed to cause a reduction in pain. Take a cold shower to encourage the release of this hormone as it will help you relax better and you will feel happy once again.

45. Get Enough Sleep

Failure to get enough sleep prevents your nerve receptors from working. Anytime this happens, whatever hurts you will hurt deeply. Make sure to get proper and adequate sleep so that you won't be amplifying the pain. In addition, sleeping adequately is crucial in the bone formation. Most of your bones are formed when you sleep, so if you are not getting the desired result, it means you lack enough rest, which is also going to slow down bone renewal.

46. Don't skip that get-together

The social occurrence has a positive cause on your natural pain reduction complex. When you spend quality time with people you like, it reduces the feelings of pain.

This means a good conversation is much better than just a distraction from pain. It physically reduces it. The part of the human brain that is stimulated by drug inclination is also stimulated by human interaction. I guess you could say we're all dependent on one another. Fortunately, having a nice time with others is a natural high with zero harm of fatal overdose.

47. Take a Warm Bath

Using of warm water increases the synthesis of beta-endorphins that are shown to improve one's mood, while also decreasing pain response. Both cold and hot water decreases pain. So, you can take a hot shower, or you should run a nice hot bath, and breathe a sigh of relief.

48. Make Sure You Eat Delicious Foods

Research has shown that eating foods pleasing to the taste bud stimulate the mu-opioid receptors, which is part of the body's reward circuit. Although we often go for unhealthy food choice due to our bodies desire for rich foods. Studies made on women reveals that after eating sweet pleasing foods they experience lesser pain.

49. Eat spicy foods

Spicy foods such as cayenne pepper and chilies pepper contain a compound called capsaicin that has been long founded to reduce pain.

Final Note

Your Enkephalin level has been directly related to your ability to withstand pain, which can also directly or indirectly affect your happy mood. Ensure you try out all these ways to increase its release and you will have yourself to thank.

6. PHENYLETHYLAMINE (PEA)

Phenethylamine supplement powder or phenylethylamine is a trace monoamine found in all plants and all animals that act as a promoter of norepinephrine and dopamine release. It is a strong mood-lift and it helps to increase endurance and attention or focus. It helps to increase learning ability and contributes to runner's high.

Phenethylamine increases serotonin and dopamine in the brain, and it may elevate a positive mood and lead to a better and greater sense of well-being and contentment. Depressed or bored individuals frequently have decreased phenylethylamine levels.

Phenethylamine is also linked to emotional sensitivity whereby it increases one's sexual drive and it is often referred to as the "love drug". Phenethylamine promotes weight loss by curbing the craving for food.

How to Release the Happy Hormone "Phenethylamine"

50. Exercise

Exercise normally decreases depression or boredom and it has been linked to increased phenethylamine.

As such, phenethylamine can also be responsible for the cause, which is known as "runner's high."

51. Eating Chocolate and Other Foods

Phenethylamine is found in chocolate, most especially dark chocolate. It is also seen in fermented foods including some certain red wines, sausage, and cheeses. Phenethylamine may be used to show food quality and freshness since bacteria produce large amounts of phenethylamine.

The phenethylamine in chocolate can explain its name or reputation as an aphrodisiac. Moreover, chocolate desire can help to "self-medicate," improving mood and increasing phenethylamine levels.

Chocolate also has little amounts of other stimulants like theobromine and caffeine. These could also be trusted for the mood-improving cause.

52. Phenethylamine Supplements

Phenethylamine's effectiveness is reduced when you use oral

supplement because it is broken down rapidly in the body by the monoamine oxidase enzyme.

Dosage of Phenylethylamine

The dosage of Phenylethylamine is suggested at around 100-500mg early in the morning or 30-40mins before exercise.

Final Note

Phenethylamine has several functions in our bodies as it contributes to the overall well-being of the body. It can be gotten either through natural foods or via supplements. In addition, with a regular dose of exercise, you will ensure that phenethylamine is released in your body to boost your happiness level.

7. GABA (Gamma Amino butyric acid)

GABA is an anti-anxiety molecule, which is an important neurotransmitter in your brain. It decreases nerve transmission by giving your neurons more time to recover. GABA neurotransmitter reduces anxiety and thereby creates a sense of calmness. It also enhances your focus and helps you maintain control.

GABA's natural purpose is to decrease the activity of the nerve cell to which it binds. In addition, it inhibits and restrains nerve transmission in the brain. This can provide a sense of wellbeing while making someone feel more peaceful and happy.

How does GABA work?

The nervous system is made up of individual nerve cells, which are called neurons. All they do is to serve as the body's wiring. The nerve indicators are transmitted through the length of a nerve cells or neurons as an electrical impulse.

For individuals with low GABA levels in the brain, increasing the accessibility of this neurotransmitter may improve factors associated with mood and health.

Abnormal heart rhythms, overly elevated moods, hyperactive excitation, insomnia, anxiety, depression, and drug/alcohol dependence are all signs that you have a deficiency of GABA molecule in your body.

Extremely low GABA levels have already been reported in teenagers diagnosed with a condition, which is called "Anhedonia." This condition is characterized by the inability to experience happiness and pleasure, even with acts that are normally related with delight and pleasure, like sex.

GABA is lower in those with panic disorders than in those without them. However, naturally raising GABA levels may improve symptoms of social anxiety and decrease the risk of anxiety episodes.

When you experience long-term insomnia, then you have low GABA levels. Because research has proven that deficiencies in GABA affect sleeping patterns. GABA helps to direct and regulate body rhythms, like sleeping, hunger, heartbeat, and others.

How to Increase GABA (Gamma Amino Butyric Acid) Levels

53. Meditation

Practicing yoga and meditation helps to increase GABA molecule in the brain and you feel more calm and happy after releasing this molecule in sufficient amount.

54. Eat glutamate-rich foods

Gamma Amino Butyric Acid is made from the neurotransmitter glutamate that is in the brain. To increase levels of Gamma Amino Butyric Acid through the diet, it is important and useful to eat glutamate-rich food sources. The foods that are high in glutamate include halibut, oranges, oats, potatoes, walnuts bananas, almonds, lentils, rice bran, and spinach to name a few.

When you want to eat foods, which are high in glutamate, you may also increase your intake of minerals, magnesium, vitamins, and the amino acids Taurine and L-Theanine.

55. Take herbal substance

Different herbal substances either assist in increasing GABA naturally or interact with GABA receptors or molecules. Some of the herbal substance includes Lemon Balm, Valerian, etc.

56. Take GABA supplements

GABA capsules can be administered directly as an oral supplement; nonetheless, there is some debate on the efficacy of supplements for increasing the level of GABA in the brain. There are proofs that when orally administered, this amino acid does not usually penetrate the Blood-Brain Barrier.

This means that if you take GABA in pill form, the chemical cannot actively reach your brain where it is needed to produce an anti-anxiety and emotional response.

Final Note

GABA is an effective neurotransmitter which helps to reduce stress and thereby makes you more relaxed and happy. Most of the time, we eat food GABA is released unconsciously, but it's time we are aware of what we eat and why we eat it in order to trigger the release of more of this neurotransmitter.

6. NOREPINEPHRINE

Norepinephrine is also known as noradrenaline. It is a substance released significantly from the ends of nerve fibers.

The rush of adrenaline is attributed to norepinephrine molecule that is why it's called the energy molecule. Norepinephrine is a stress hormone involved in the fight or flight response, whereby the body is ready to retreat to or react from an urgent threat.

Its presence set the tone for many of the physical components of emotion such as cognition, decision-making, increased heart rate, and alertness.

The blood pressure is further increased by norepinephrine because of its causes and effects on the heart muscle, thereby increasing the output of blood from the heart. Norepinephrine also acts to increase blood glucose levels and free fatty acids. This substance has been shown to adjust the purpose of particular types of immune cells (e.g., T cells).

Norepinephrine is used clinically as a means of maintaining blood pressure in the shock related case such as septic shock.

Norepinephrine helps mood deficiency of serotonin and helps to prevent depression. Norepinephrine has effects on individual behavior such as modulation of vigilance, attention, reward, arousal, motivation, and learning.

Norepinephrine also plays a role in cognitive and memory function as it improves processing of sensation inputs, improves formation, improves attention and retrieval of both working and long-term memory, and also improve the power of the brain to make respond to inputs by changing the activity pattern in the prefrontal internal organ and other areas.

Norepinephrine is believed to cure chronic fatigue syndrome. Norepinephrine also helps to alleviate migraines and make you feel better after a while.

How to Increase Norepinephrine

57. Rigorous exercise

Rigorous exercise helps to improve your level of norepinephrine by improving your cardiovascular system and triggering the release of the substance.

58. Eating balanced meal

Ensure you eat balanced meals containing whole grains, lean protein, and vegetables.

Final Note

With a balanced meal combined with exercise, you will

definitely trigger the release of this happy hormone. Aside from this, you will also enjoy a sound health when you feed and exercise well.

7. SEROTONIN

Serotonin is one of the most general and widely recognized neurotransmitters in the body. It is involved in many core physical processes such as the regulation of aggression, appetite, and sleep. Serotonin is also an important key player in anxiety, fear, a general sense of well-being and mood. Imbalances in serotonin, specifically relevant to dopamine and norepinephrine, are common effects and causes of certain types of depression.

Antidepressants that block serotonin's re-absorption back into serotonin nerve cells are in the midst of the most common and usual of all classes of medications prescribed.

Serotonin deficiency is a usual and common contributor to mood problems. Some people feel it is a widespread disease in the US.

Serotonin contributes to our happy mood and is very useful for our emotions because it defends against depression and anxiety.

What contributes to Serotonin Deficiency?

Many of the things that stress one in life can be attributed to low serotonin levels and extended periods of stress can cause a reduction in the body's serotonin levels. Faulty metabolism, digestive issues, and genetic factors contribute to these imbalances. The improper breakdown of our food can impair absorption that reduces our capacity to build serotonin.

Poor diet is also a known cause of low serotonin levels, as you do not take in enough vitamins, protein, or minerals to build the neurotransmitters, hence, a neurotransmitter imbalance develops. So, we really need to think about what we eat.

Toxic substances like drug use, pesticides, heavy metals, and some prescription drugs can have an effect and cause permanent damage to the neuron that makes serotonin and other neurotransmitters.

Certain substances and drug such as alcohol, NutraSweet, nicotine, antidepressants, caffeine, and some medications that lower cholesterol reduces the level of serotonin and other neurotransmitters.

Hormonal changes affect and cause low serotonin level and neurotransmitter imbalances. Lack of sunlight can also contribute to low serotonin levels.

Serotonin helps to tighten smooth muscles and transmit nerve cell impulses as it regulates body processes and contributes to the overall well-being and happiness.

FUNCTIONS OF SEROTONIN

As a neurotransmitter and a hormone, serotonin affects the majority of brain cells. The following is a list of things that serotonin could affect.

1. Mood.

It is well-known for its role in the brain where it plays a major part in mood, emotions, feelings, anxiety, and happiness.

2. Nausea.

When you eat something that is toxic or irritating which might lead to vomiting, more serotonin is produced in the gut to increase transit time and expel the irritant in diarrhea. The reduction in serotonin level in the blood leads to cases of nausea.

3. Sexual function.

Research shows that low serotonin levels which come as a result of intoxication contribute to the increase in libido and sexual function, while those taking serotonin-inducing medication are seen to have a reduction in libido and sexual function.

Symptoms of Serotonin Deficiency

You may have a deficiency of serotonin if you have a low energy, feel tense, harbor negative thoughts, possess a depressed mood, craving for sweets, irritable, and have a reduced interest in sex. Some other serotonin-related disorders include:

Anxiety

Insomnia

Depression

Panic Attacks

PMS/ Hormone dysfunction

Irritable Bowel

Obesity

Compulsions and Obsession

Fibromyalgia

Eating disorders

Migraine Headaches

Alcohol abuse

Chronic pain

How to Increase the Happy Hormone "Serotonin"

Serotonin is likely to depreciate in its level, which is because of depression and anxiety

Under listed are ways to increase the serotonin level.

59. Eat food rich in vitamin B6

Since you must acquire and get this important and useful vitamin from your foods (or supplements), these are some vitamin B6-rich options: turnip greens, cauliflower, garlic, mustard greens, celery, spinach, fish (halibut, cod, salmon, especially tuna, and snapper), poultry (turkey and chicken) and lean beef tenderloin.

60. Eat high protein meals

Focus on food combination and digestion when you eat foods that are high in protein – and particularly have a higher percentage of tryptophan (like sunflower seeds, pumpkin seeds, and turkey), they will provide the needed precursor of serotonin, which is tryptophan. However, beware, as research shows that eating carbohydrates with protein actually works against your capacity to make serotonin.

Final Note

Serotonin is a major happy hormone in the body. It has many functions as well as its sources in the body. Its deficiency can cause a lot of damage to health. Therefore, it is expedient that ways to increase it need to be stuck to and practiced well for the general benefit of your health.

SUMMARY

True happiness is a goal of everyone as no one wants to live a miserable life filled with regret, depression, fear, and anxiety. We all need to feel loved and cared for as we crave the attention of others.

While discussing ways to release these happy hormones, some factors stand out which are exercise, food, and spending time with friends. Doing what you love doing is a sure way to be happy in life.

True happiness cannot be achieved without a change of habit and lifestyle. However, you need to identify those habits you have that have been contributing to the emotional state you find yourself right now. Without identifying it and making a decision to correct it, your bid to be happy will be an exercise in futility. We have also discovered that certain hormones actually contribute to our level of happiness. Smart people learn how to release these hormones to benefit their emotional state and improve their overall well-being.

Therefore, the next time you want to eat that fatty food, think about it, does it trigger any happy hormones in you or will it affect your mood in the end.

Take your pen and writing materials. Write out ten habits you have and try to evaluate if it contributes to your happiness or not. If your answer is NO, then you need to find a way to strike it out or replace the habit with a better one. While doing this, you will definitely enjoy a mood lift and happiness will flow in easily.

CONCLUSION

Happiness is a by-product of our emotions. Happiness has grade and levels; it ranges from being contented to intense joy.

You cannot afford not to live happy as you only have one life to do so. Though happiness is a choice, it's an obvious choice among many other choices.

While there are several other hormones that contribute to happiness, the ones mentioned in this book are the major ones which you need to watch out for and learn ways to release.

Interestingly, happiness is linked to our health. When you are happy, you will be healthy, this is because they both come from the same root which is our mind. You experience a feeling of joy when neurotransmitters are being released by your brain.

We have discussed how your brain triggers the release of happy hormones and how it is increased in the body.

True happiness cannot be achieved without a correspondent change in attitude and lifestyle. Do not allow life circumstances or situations to affect your happiness because you will be damaging your health by doing so.

You cannot do the same thing repeatedly in the same way and expect a different result. It doesn't work that way. This is time for a paradigm shift. Apply what you have learned here. So, to be happy in life you need to start doing things differently in the right way and happiness will definitely come. I wish you a fulfilled and happy life because you deserve it!